LOVE
LIKE YOU'VE
NEVER BEEN
HURT

LOVE
LIKE YOU'VE NEVER BEEN
HURT
PARTICIPANT'S GUIDE

HOPE, HEALING
AND THE
POWER OF AN OPEN HEART

JENTEZEN FRANKLIN

WITH **CHERISE FRANKLIN**
AND **A. J. GREGORY**

Chosen
a division of Baker Publishing Group
Minneapolis, Minnesota

Published by Chosen Books
11400 Hampshire Avenue South
Bloomington, Minnesota 55438
www.chosenbooks.com

Chosen Books is a division of
Baker Publishing Group, Grand Rapids, Michigan

Printed in the United States of America

ISBN 978-0-8007-9909-0

Cover design by LOOK Design Studio

Author is represented by The FEDD Agency, Inc.

18   19   20   21   22   23   24   7   6   5   4   3

CONTENTS

A NOTE FROM PASTOR JENTEZEN

I will never forget the day I sat in my study and read the words legendary pitcher Satchel Paige is reported to have said: "Work like you don't need the money. Love like you've never been hurt. Dance like nobody's watching."

The part that struck me, of course, was "love like you've never been hurt." To me, that is a profound statement. If you're human, you're going to get hurt. As sure as you are holding this book in your hand, someone has offended you (or will). Someone has rejected you (or will). Someone has lied to you (or will). Someone has disappointed you (or will). Someone has let you down (or will). As you read these words, you might be nursing a wound or staring at a scar. You might be thinking of a relationship you cut off because someone you loved hurt you deeply. Maybe you had a terrible injustice done to you that you cannot get past.

Here's the thing: Jesus warned us offenses would come. He said, "It is impossible that no offenses should come, but woe to him through whom they do come!" (Luke 17:1). While getting hurt is part of life, the more important thing is how we deal with it. See, some of us hold on for dear life to the pain that comes from getting hurt. Choosing not to forgive hinders our walk with God and our relationships with others. It keeps us stuck. It can even make us physically sick.

If you allow the wounds and hurts and cuts of others to trap you in the place where you become bitter, you will lose the wonder of Christianity. You will lose your joy. You will not have peace. Unforgiveness that is not addressed leads to great bitterness, which will drain you of mental, emotional, spiritual and physical power. When you use up all your energy thinking about negative situations—the person who always gossips about you, getting let go from your job—you sabotage your success in life. And when your world is overwhelmed by heartbreak or unwarranted pain, if you do not allow God to heal you, you will not become who He has called you to be.

Let me be clear: I am not denying your wounds are real. If you have been abused, let down or abandoned, it hurts, I know. And it is hard, sometimes painfully hard, to work through. But listen carefully. While your pain is real, we serve a God who will never allow our wounds to get deadly.

Forgiveness is the cure. Without forgiveness, you will not have peace. You will live in a constant state of unease and tension. It matters more what happens in us than what happens to us. God is saying to you right now, "Let go so you can take hold."

I want to invite you on an adventure of loving like you've never been hurt. Healing awaits. Freedom awaits. Great peace awaits. But it depends on you.

I am very excited that you are holding this book in your hand. My prayer is that God reveals the areas in your life you need to reset through the power of forgiveness, and that you invite Him to begin to heal you. A fruitful life is not an accident. It is a result of right choices. If you choose to forgive, forgiveness can rewrite your future!

Whether you are a seasoned Christian or brand-new to the faith, this guide will help you let go of the past to lay hold of the future. It's time to restart your heart.

HOW TO USE THIS GUIDE

This participant's guide is designed for you to work through in a group setting or on your own. It is also formatted to work in conjunction with my book *Love Like You've Never Been Hurt* and the video teaching that accompanies it. But don't worry if you have not read the book or won't get a chance to watch the video sessions. You will find plenty of content here that will help you begin, today, to make great change happen in your life and in your relationships.

This participant's guide is divided into six sessions that each include the following:

- A big idea to introduce the overall message of the session
- A start-up segment that sets the stage for the video session and the discussion to follow
- Notes and a set of in-depth group discussion questions drawn from the video session
- A set of in-depth group discussion questions drawn from the Bible, my book and real-life matters
- A closing prayer
- A reflection and action segment to be completed on your own time

If you want to dive deeper and maximize your experience outside of your small group, spend time in the "Personal Reflection" and "Personal Action" portions at the end of each session. There may be things you are not ready to share with others in your small group, so you can use this segment in a more private manner as well as a more practical way. I encourage you to use this opportunity to reflect on what you have learned and on what God has been speaking to you about.

What You'll Need

Unless otherwise marked, all the Scriptures in this guide are offered in the New King James Version (NKJV). If you prefer a different version, have a Bible or Bible app handy to look up the verses in the translation of your choice. While not required (as space is provided in this guide), consider using a journal or digital device to jot down notes or anything that speaks to you. Finally, while you do not have to do this, you will get the most out of this guide if you read *Love Like You've Never Been Hurt.*

Follow the schedule below to coordinate with this participant's guide:

Read	Watch	Discuss
Introduction and chapters 1, 2 and 3 of *Love Like You've Never Been Hurt*	Video session 1	Session 1, "Love Always Wins"
Chapter 4	Video session 2	Session 2, "Engage the Power of Forgiveness"
Chapters 5, 6 and 7	Video session 3	Session 3, "Love Well"
Chapters 8, 9, 10 and 11	Video session 4	Session 4, "Build Up and Fight for Your Marriage and Family"
Chapter 12	Video session 5	Session 5, "Love God Even When It Hurts"
Chapters 13 and 14	Video session 6	Session 6, "Restart Your Heart"

I am excited to see how God is going to open wide your heart to love like you've never been hurt.

LOVE ALWAYS WINS

Big Idea for This Session

The ones you love the most can hurt you the most. Love them anyway. Love people who have messed up, too. You do not compromise when you choose to love. Love never fails.

Session Start-Up

A story is told about Muhammad Ali on an airplane flight. Before taking off, the flight attendant noticed his seat belt was unbuckled. "Please fasten your seat belt, Mr. Ali," she told him. Ali looked at her and smiled. "Superman don't need no seat belt," he said. Without even blinking, the flight attendant retorted, "Superman don't need no airplane. Now, please fasten your seat belt."

None of us are Superman or Wonder Woman. We are vulnerable. We have weaknesses. We all go through tough times. Many of our difficulties and trials revolve around relationships. You might be married and are having trouble in paradise. You might be a parent struggling with a wayward child. You might be caught in a sibling rivalry that cut you off from your sister, so that you haven't spoken in twenty years. Maybe you severed your relationship with your best friend because she said some horrible things about you. Maybe you were abandoned by someone entrusted to care for you.

It is hard to love in these instances, but that is what God has called us to do—love, at all times and in all circumstances. Jesus said, "Your love for one another will prove to the world that you are my disciples" (John 13:35). Jesus did not say we would be recognized as His followers by what we wear or don't wear, how much education we have, how much theology we know or how many rules we follow. The standard is love.

There are only two subjects in the Bible that God thinks are important enough to ascribe an entire chapter to: one, faith (see Hebrews 11), and two, love (see 1 Corinthians 13). In the latter chapter, Paul writes, "Love never fails. But whether there are prophecies, they will fail; whether there are tongues, they will cease; whether there is knowledge, it will vanish away" (1 Corinthians 13:8).

In this chapter, we see that love even trumps the power gifts of the Spirit. It's not that they are unnecessary but that the priority is love. Love never fails. It is the greatest gift.

God looked at a world held captive by Satan and demonic powers, and He said, "I know how I can combat that!" He then unleashed His greatest weapon, love. If God could save the world with His Son, Jesus Christ, then we need to get a revelation. If we want change in our lives, in our hearts and in our relationships, we need to begin to love on a new level.

When we choose to love even though we've been hurt, even though others have made mistakes, even though we feel someone does not deserve it, we begin to love the way God loves. Without condition. Without expectation. No strings attached.

Talk about It

There are countless definitions of the word *love*. In what way or by what measure do you define it?

Video Session 1

Watch video session 1. While viewing the video, use the space below to record key ideas or any thoughts you want to remember.

Video Teaching Notes

If you are going to hold your relationships together, it is going to require forgiveness. God requires of us what He does for us. He loves us like we've never hurt Him.

You don't just need a good memory. You need a good forgettery.

All of us have been shot. Get in the truck and drive.

Have you gone through something that offends you and hurts you badly? If you will let God heal you of your wound, your darkest night will be like daytime, and the sun will shine seven times brighter (see Isaiah 30:26).

Love never fails.

It's never wrong to love.

Video Discussion

1. Think about the story I told of President James Garfield. Do you have a wound that you keep reopening and reliving? Is it making you stuck in life?

2. Do we ever have the right *not* to love someone?

3. What does it mean to be a minister of reconciliation?

Small-Group Discussion

1. God's love for us is universal. It is unchanging. It is not based on our performance. It is not based on how many times we go to church. It is not based on how much we tithe—or if we do at all. It is not based on how faithful we are to Him. God loves us because He is love.

We read in Ephesians 5:1–2, "Therefore be imitators of God as dear children. And walk in love, as Christ also has loved us and given Himself for us, an offering and a sacrifice to God for a sweet-smelling aroma." Give an example of how you can put this scriptural command into action daily.

2. It is easy to love people when we share the same ideologies, the same politics, the same lifestyle, the same theology, the same values. It is harder to love those with whom we differ. Share about a time when you were challenged to love someone who was different from you in opinions, beliefs or values. How did you put love into action despite these differences? If this was a challenge for you, how can you handle a similar relationship in the future?

3. Talk about a time in which God comforted you when someone betrayed you, offended you, lied to you, rejected you or broke your heart. Can you offer Scripture you took to heart during this time?

4. Love involves trust. But what happens when someone we know or love has repeatedly broken our trust? In what ways can we practice loving from a distance?

5. Has your idea of loving others who hurt you changed over the years? Why or why not?

6. Isaiah 30:26 gives those of us who need healing from hurtful situations hope: "Moreover the light of the moon will be as the light of the sun, and the light of the sun will be sevenfold, as the light of seven days, in the day that the LORD binds up the bruise of His people and heals the stroke of their wound." How does this Scripture encourage you to pursue healing, release the past and move into a future of wholeness?

7. On pages 43–45 of *Love Like You've Never Been Hurt*, the story is told about a father, Mac, and his teenage son, Malcolm. As a Christian, Mac is shocked to learn that his son is homosexual. After having time to process the revelation, Mac said, "I knew I couldn't push him away or push my beliefs on him. All I needed to do was to give my son to God, pray for him and love him. I don't condemn him for his lifestyle. It's not my place. I simply love him."

Talk about a situation in which someone close to you was not living the way he or she ought to be living. What did your relationship with that person look like? How did you love the person despite his or her lifestyle choices? What boundaries, if any, did you set?

Bonus Questions

8. Is it difficult for you to share or be vulnerable with others because of the hurt you have experienced? Maybe you have opened up in the past and someone betrayed that confidence. What holds you back from sharing with others?

9. In Matthew 5:44 Jesus told us, "Love your enemies." Talk about setting the bar high! You might be wondering if this is even possible, especially if you have been hurt on a deep level. Or maybe you have experienced true forgiveness and God has healed your heart in such a transformative way that you have lived this mandate out. Give an example of how we can love our enemies.

10. Lamentations 3:22–23 promises, "Through the Lord's mercies we are not consumed, because His compassions fail not. They are new every morning; great is Your faithfulness." Meditate on this verse for a moment.

   This should encourage you to show mercy, kindness and love to those who have failed, who have made mistakes, who are not living right. While setting healthy boundaries may be necessary in certain situations, we must learn to reflect in others the kind of love God has for us. When you are tempted to judge, criticize or cut people down for falling short in their faith or in their relationships with you, how can this Scripture help you to extend mercy?

_____

_____

_____

_____

_____

Wrap-Up

Today we have learned how powerful love is. It can shatter division and rebuild what has been broken. Let's take a deep breath and close our time in prayer. Here are some ideas from this session that can guide our conversation with God:

- Thank God for His amazing love that knows no bounds, that is limitless, unchanging and pure.
- Pray for God to reveal areas in your life where you need healing because of something someone has done to you. Ask Him to begin to change your heart and your mind.
- Ask the Holy Spirit to soften your heart and teach you how to love others instead of judge them. Pray for opportunities to imitate God's love.
- Offer to God the relationship(s) that have been broken because of offenses. Ask Him to begin the process of healing and, wherever possible, reconciliation.

Prepare for the Next Session

Before the group meets again, read chapter 4 in *Love Like You've Never Been Hurt*.

BETWEEN SESSIONS

Personal Reflection

1. I have said that family provides us with our greatest joys and at times our deepest sorrows. If you are married, think about the greatest joys you have experienced with your spouse and/or your children. The spontaneous moments of romance. The family vacations filled with play and fun. The powerful times you prayed together and witnessed the answers. The moment your teenager asked you for advice. Write them down in the space below.

   If you are not married or don't have children, think about the ones you love most. Consider your siblings, your parents, your best friends. Write down heartwarming memories with these individuals.

It may be more painful to think about the tough times. You may not want to admit to your scars or even your open wounds. Maybe you don't want anyone to find out your son struggles with depression or a daughter struggles with an addiction. Maybe you are ashamed because you had an affair or heartbroken because you just found out your spouse has. Spend time in prayer today and admit the challenge(s) you face in your relationships. In the space below, write down what you want God to accomplish in your life and the life of your loved ones as you read through this participant's guide.

_____

_____

_____

_____

_____

_____

_____

_____

2. Paul writes in Philippians 3:13–14,

> I do not count myself to have apprehended; but one thing I do, forgetting those things which are behind and reaching forward to those things which are ahead, I press toward the goal for the prize of the upward call of God in Christ Jesus.

In other words, to move forward, you have to let go of the past. You have to release what is behind you and reach for what is before you. Take time and reflect on what you need to let go of so you can move forward in your life.

_____

_____

----

3. Read 1 Corinthians 13:

Though I speak with the tongues of men and of angels, but have not love, I have become sounding brass or a clanging cymbal. And though I have the gift of prophecy, and understand all mysteries and all knowledge, and though I have all faith, so that I could remove mountains, but have not love, I am nothing. And though I bestow all my goods to feed the poor, and though I give my body to be burned, but have not love, it profits me nothing.

Love suffers long and is kind; love does not envy; love does not parade itself, is not puffed up; does not behave rudely, does not seek its own, is not provoked, thinks no evil; does not rejoice in iniquity, but rejoices in the truth; bears all things, believes all things, hopes all things, endures all things.

Love never fails. But whether there are prophecies, they will fail; whether there are tongues, they will cease; whether there is knowledge, it will vanish away. For we know in part and we prophesy in part. But when that which is perfect has come, then that which is in part will be done away.

When I was a child, I spoke as a child, I understood as a child, I thought as a child; but when I became a man, I put away childish things. For now we see in a mirror, dimly, but then face to face. Now I know in part, but then I shall know just as I also am known.

And now abide faith, hope, love, these three; but the greatest of these is love.

Highlight the phrases or statements that move you. Write down why.

Personal Action

Martin Luther King Jr. wrote, "Love is the only force capable of transforming an enemy into a friend."* That's powerful! Think about someone in your family with whom you have had a disagreement or an intense confrontation that led to a separation of sorts. Maybe you have not talked for months. Maybe you slid off the radar because you did not approve of the way that person is living. Maybe the person is ashamed of something that happened and has been avoiding your calls.

Take time today to pray for that person and that relationship. Seek God's direction on how to show love. Think of ways you can make this happen. Knock on his door. Invite her out to dinner. Pick up the phone and say, "I'm sorry." Send an email wishing that person well.

You've got nothing to lose. After all, love never fails.

*Martin Luther King Jr., "Martin Luther King, Jr. on Loving Your Enemies," *OnFaith*, accessed November 8, 2017, https://www.onfaith.co/onfaith/2015/01/19/martin-luther-king -jr-on-loving-your-enemies/35907.

ENGAGE THE POWER OF FORGIVENESS

Big Idea for This Session

Stop keeping score and start losing count. Forgive—everybody and always.

Session Start-Up

Life is an adventure in forgiving. Or, at least, it should be. While we all have different talents and skill sets, I've found that many of us are really good at one thing—keeping count when people hurt us. Instead of forgiving others, we tally their offenses and, in the process, we invite unforgiveness into our hearts. It sits. It festers. Often, like a tumor, it grows. No doubt, unforgiveness is a sickness.

Jesus gives two big reasons why we should forgive people who have wounded us. One, He said, "For if you forgive men their trespasses, your heavenly Father will also forgive you" (Matthew 6:14). In other words, forgive, and God will forgive you. Don't forgive, and God won't forgive you.

Two, unforgiveness opens the door to torment. Jesus wrapped up the parable of the unforgiving servant with this warning: "And his master was angry, and delivered him to the torturers until he should pay all that was due to him. So My heavenly Father also will do to you if each of you, from his heart, does not forgive his brother his trespasses" (Matthew 18:34–35). Unforgiveness does a great deal more damage to the vessel it's stored in than the object on which it is poured. Torment can only be healed by releasing forgiveness.

Forgiveness is powerful. It unleashes the Spirit of God. It is the key that will unlock the doors of heaven and usher in peace, blessing and joy. Jesus said, "Whatever you bind on earth will be bound in heaven, and whatever you loose on earth will be loosed in heaven" (Matthew 18:18). You can split hell wide open by releasing forgiveness.

There are many myths about forgiveness that I shatter in my book and which I will talk about in the video session. The important thing to remember is that no matter how badly we have been hurt or how terrible the offense, Jesus calls us to forgive. Not just one time, but all the time. We may not feel like it. It might be hard. It might take time. We might have to do it over and over again. But we cannot afford not to forgive. It's a choice we must make to be the people God is calling us to be.

Forgiveness is like a flashlight. No matter how dark it seems to get, it will help you find your way again.

Talk about It

Why do you think forgiving others is so hard for some people?

Video Session 2

Watch video session 2. While viewing the video, use the space below to record key ideas or any thoughts you want to remember.

Video Teaching Notes

Jesus told us to forgive seventy times seven.

Forgiveness is not about keeping score; it's about losing count.

Sometimes it takes the worst things done to you to bring out the best in you.

It takes opposition to give you wings to soar.

The storm will not take you out; it will bring you up.

It is unforgivable not to forgive.

Tap and keep on tapping. Ask and keep on asking. Seek and keep on seeking. Knock and keep on knocking.

Video Discussion

1. What can you do to remind yourself to forgive "seventy times seven"—or, all of the time?

2. How has opposition given you the opportunity to rise above?

3. How do we give ourselves over to the enemy's tormentors?

_____

_____

_____

_____

_____

_____

Small-Group Discussion

1. Read the following Scriptures out loud:

   - Matthew 6:12: "And forgive us our debts, as we forgive our debtors."
   - Ephesians 4:32: "And be kind to one another, tenderhearted, forgiving one another, even as God in Christ forgave you."
   - Colossians 3:13: "Bearing with one another, and forgiving one another, if anyone has a complaint against another; even as Christ forgave you, so you also must do."

   What is the fundamental spiritual truth God is telling you through His Word? How can the significance of this truth help you navigate through your current relationships?

2. When we are unwilling to forgive someone who offended or hurt us, how does that choice affect us emotionally, spiritually,

mentally or physically? Share an example in which you forgave someone and felt released from inner torment.

3. Describe a time when you struggled with forgiving someone. What held you back from releasing the person who hurt you? What ultimately motivated you to choose to forgive?

4. A challenge many of us have is determining the boundaries of forgiveness. This is the issue Peter was getting at when he asked Jesus, "Lord, how often shall my brother sin against me, and I forgive him? Up to seven times?" (Matthew 18:21).

   Are there boundaries to forgiveness? Is there any point in a relationship at which it is right to cut ties with someone who hurt you?

5. Forgiveness for some can be a process. Even after forgiving someone, either face-to-face or in your heart, you can experience residual anger, bitterness or sadness. This might indicate further healing is necessary.

   If this is true for you today, how can you continue the healing process so you are not triggered by the events of the past?

6. In *Love Like You've Never Been Hurt*, I offer some insight into what forgiveness is *not*:
   - Forgiveness does not mean you forget what happened.
   - Forgiveness does not release the offender from consequences.
   - Forgiveness does not always mean reconciliation.

   If you are having a hard time forgiving someone, how can these truths move you toward forgiveness?

7. Genesis 37–45 tells the story of Joseph, a man who was tossed into a pit and sold into slavery by his own brothers. After being brought to Egypt, he ended up working in Potiphar's palace, where he was falsely accused of rape and thrown into prison.

After serving many years for a crime he did not commit, through a series of God-ordained events, Joseph became a ruler in Egypt. It was during this time that he came once again face-to-face with his brothers. All the lands were suffering from a terrible famine, but Egypt still had food, thanks to Joseph. His brothers showed up at the palace and, not knowing his true identity, begged Joseph for food. When Joseph revealed himself, his brothers were afraid. In perhaps one of the most powerful acts of forgiveness in the Bible, Joseph said to them, "But now, do not therefore be grieved or angry with yourselves because you sold me here; for God sent me before you to preserve life" (Genesis 45:5). If you were Joseph, what would you have said to your brothers?

_____

_____

_____

_____

_____

_____

_____

_____

_____

_____

Bonus Questions

8. Often, it is not other people we have trouble forgiving but ourselves. If you are still beating yourself up over something God has already forgiven you for, what can you do, starting today, to begin to forgive yourself and move on?

9. Romans 12:19–21 says,

> Beloved, do not avenge yourselves, but rather give place to wrath; for it is written, "Vengeance is Mine, I will repay," says the Lord. Therefore "If your enemy is hungry, feed him; if he is thirsty, give him a drink; for in so doing you will heap coals of fire on his head." Do not be overcome by evil, but overcome evil with good.

Think of a way you can overcome evil with good instead of seeking revenge on someone who hurt you.

10. What kind of people do you find it most difficult to forgive and why?

_____

_____

_____

_____

_____

Wrap-Up

Today we have learned about the power of forgiveness. If we want to live healed and whole and walk in the path God has called us to, we must engage in a lifestyle of forgiveness. Jesus is very clear that if we do not forgive others, He will not forgive us. When we release the power of forgiveness, we release the power of God to work in our lives.

Let's close our time together in prayer. Here are some ideas from this session that can guide our conversation with God:

- Thank God for dying on the cross for you and for forgiving you of all your sins.

- Ask the Holy Spirit to soften your heart toward others, especially toward someone who has offended or hurt you.
- Pray for God to search your heart and bring to mind anything you may have done to another person that warrants your asking that person for forgiveness.
- Ask God to remind you of His continual grace and mercy so you can show grace and mercy to others.

Prepare for the Next Session

Before the group meets again, read chapters 5, 6 and 7 in *Love Like You've Never Been Hurt*.

BETWEEN SESSIONS

Personal Reflection

1. Another powerful act of forgiveness takes place between David and King Saul in the Old Testament. Here is the backdrop of this story: Saul was so jealous of David, his protégé, that he had determined to kill David, and David went into hiding to save his own skin. He had been on the run from King Saul for many years when King Saul got some encouraging intel about where David was hiding. The king took several thousand soldiers with him and headed toward the desert. Unbeknownst to Saul, David lurked in the shadows of the very cave Saul had used to take a break. It was a golden opportunity for David to take out the unsuspecting king. But he didn't. Instead, he crept stealthily toward Saul and sliced off a piece of his robe. Saul never heard or saw a thing.

   While holding on to the scrap of material, David felt guilty. After Saul walked out, David fell on his knees out of respect and called out to the king.

Why do you listen to the words of men who say, "Indeed David seeks your harm"? Look, this day your eyes have seen that the LORD delivered you today into my hand in the cave, and someone urged me to kill you. But my eye spared you. . . . Know and see that there is neither evil nor rebellion in my hand, and I have not sinned against you. Yet you hunt my life to take it. Let the LORD judge between you and me, and let the LORD avenge me on you. But my hand shall not be against you. . . . Therefore let the LORD be judge, and judge between you and me, and see and plead my case, and deliver me out of your hand.

1 Samuel 24:9–12, 15

Wow! Fifteen hundred years before Jesus came on the scene, David modeled what it means to "love your enemies, bless those who curse you" (Matthew 5:44). David did not allow the power of rage, bitterness or vengeance to rule over him. We can learn much from him. A man after God's own heart, he knew it was better to trust God than take matters into his own hand.

How can this story apply to your life? Are you trying to seek revenge on someone who did you wrong? How can you start trusting God that He will deal with your offender?

2. Think about two ways in which you can develop a lifestyle of forgiving (e.g., changing your attitude or reminding yourself daily of scriptural truths).

_____

_____

_____

_____

_____

Personal Action

1. Psalm 139:23–24 tells us, "Search me, O God, and know my heart; try me, and know my anxieties; and see if there is any wicked way in me, and lead me in the way everlasting."

   Take time today or in the next few days to pray and ask God to help you look deep within your heart to find if any unforgiveness is present. You might not even need God to address the issue. You may, after working through this session, have pictured immediately the person, place or offense that has crippled you emotionally, mentally or spiritually.

   Name the person or people who have wounded you. Tell God what happened. Tell Him how it made you feel. Then ask God to forgive you of bitterness or resentment. Ask Him to forgive you for holding on to the weight of unforgiveness for so long.

   After that, release forgiveness to the person who has hurt you. Sometimes this is appropriate to do in person. Other times it is okay to do it in your heart. If you feel bound by unforgiveness and need inner healing from years of abuse or pain, I encourage you to meet with your pastor or a counselor to begin the healing process.

2. Perhaps this session is not about your needing to forgive someone but your needing to be forgiven. Use the steps below to guide this process:

   • Take responsibility for your actions.
   • Genuinely repent.
   • Correct the situation if possible.
   • Ask for forgiveness.

   Depending on your situation, this can be done through a letter, a phone call, in person or in prayer.

   These are the first steps toward freedom. Friend, it is time to let God heal your past. It is time to let Him give you a new beginning.

LOVE WELL

Big Idea for This Session

W hen you love yourself, you can love others, learn to control your emotions through the Holy Spirit and bring peace wherever you go.

Session Start-Up

Before we can love others, we must learn how to love ourselves. This is easy for some people and harder for others. Jesus emphasized the significance of this truth when He said, "'You shall love the LORD your God with all your heart, with all your soul, and with all your mind.' This is the first and great commandment. And the second is like it: 'You shall love your neighbor as yourself'" (Matthew 22:37–39). If you can't love yourself, then you won't be able to love others well. Jesus was implying that if you want a good relationship with others and with God, you must start by feeling good about yourself. This does not mean being selfish or narcissistic. It means being confident in who you are based on what *God* says about you.

When we have God esteem instead of self-esteem, we have the capacity to love others, to turn the other cheek, to be kind. That is a big one—being kind. Ever meet a mean Christian? It's not a pretty sight. How can we show the love of Jesus if we are rude, short-tempered, judgmental or irritable? Simple. We can't.

There is something Christlike about what I like to call the value of a warm place. This means that we as Christians are welcoming to whoever washes up on our shores. If they are struggling with an addiction or hurting from a divorce, we throw a warm blanket around them and say, "Come on in. Let me warm you by the fire of the Holy Spirit." Kindness will reach a lot of people. Warmth will reach a lot of people. Acceptance will reach a lot of people. We do not compromise our faith when we're kind. We're just saying to people, "Jesus loves you. I love you. You belong."

It seems that everywhere we go, we run into angry people. Sometimes we run into rage (think people cutting you off on the highway). Sometimes we run into low-grade anger. Many people are on edge, so that just about anything will tick them off. Ephesians 4:26 tells us, "Be angry, and do not sin." There is no way to never be angry, but it is possible not to sin when you are angry.

Jesus did not call us to be angry, mean or vindictive people. He called us to be peacemakers. He wants us to show up in an intense situation and, instead of adding to the tension by our presence, to bring peace. We are called to defuse volatile situations. We need to allow the Holy Spirit to work in us so that whatever circumstance we are in, we walk in the blessing of peace.

Talk about It

Is it easier to be kind and peaceful to strangers you will probably never see again or the people that you do life with? Why?

Video Session 3

Watch video session 3. While viewing the video, use the space below to record key ideas or any thoughts you want to remember.

Video Teaching Notes

If you don't love yourself, you won't know how to love anybody else.

Once you begin to see yourself as God sees you, turn around and see others the way God sees them.

Anger is not a sin; mismanaging it is.

To be kind is to be holy.

God calls us to be peacemakers, not troublemakers.

Video Discussion

1. In Acts 13, we read about Paul and Barnabas preaching to a crowd of Jewish people who would not accept their message. The reason fascinates me: It was not because of sin. It was not because of God. It was not because of Satan. *They* were the problem. Paul said that these people judged themselves unworthy (see Acts 13:46). Talk about a time when you believed you were too unworthy to receive from God.

2. What spoke to you in the story of Paul being shipwrecked and washing up on the shores of Malta? How do you deal in the area of kindness, particularly to those who have done you wrong?

3. Talk about a situation in which you can serve as a peacemaker.

Small-Group Discussion

1. Loving ourselves is rooted in who we are in God. When we are secure in who He is and how much He loves us, we can mirror that love toward others. What connections can you draw between loving yourself and loving others?

2. Talk about why it is important for Christians especially to be kind to others. How can we practice kindness when we do not feel like it, when we are tired or when the pressures of life weigh us down?

3. One way we can be intentional about being kind to others is by remembering the kindness others have shown to us. We need to take the warmth and give the warmth. Share a story of when you experienced "unusual kindness" (Acts 28:2). How did this benevolence inspire you to show unusual kindness to someone else?

4. In 1 Corinthians 13:4, Paul writes that love is "kind." The Greek word is *chrésteuomai*, which means "to show oneself useful."* What is the difference between being kind in this context and simply being nice to someone?

5. Share a time when you lost your temper. What triggered that episode? What was the aftermath, and how did you deal with it?

6. What do you think of when you read the word *peacemaker*? Tell about a person who exhibited the traits or actions you describe.

7. Genesis 27 relates the feud between brothers Jacob and Esau. After Jacob stole Esau's birthright blessing from him, the Bible tells us that "Esau hated Jacob . . . and Esau said in his heart, 'The days of mourning for my father are at hand; then I will kill my brother Jacob'" (Genesis 27:41). Why is it human nature to seek revenge on someone who caused us harm?

*Online Parallel Bible Project, "5541. chrésteuomai," Bible Hub, accessed November 15, 2017, http://biblehub.com/greek/5541.htm.

Bonus Questions

8. In *Love Like You've Never Been Hurt*, I write,

> One of the most important [lessons about kindness] is that it is better to be reconciled than to be right. Do you know how many times I slept in the guest bedroom because I was mad at Cherise for something, usually something dumb? Funny thing is, she could not have cared less. She was the one getting a good night's rest in the comfortable bed all by herself! Back in the day, heated arguments would occasionally turn ugly, peppered with unkind words and unfair accusations. . . . In many of the arguments we had early in our marriage, I would fight to the death to prove my point. I wanted her to see that I was right. But even if I "won," I paid a price for it. All it did was push her away and drive us further apart. It would have been better for me to shut up . . . and, instead, reach out to reconcile.

Share a time when you pursued the "win" in an argument at the price of hurting the relationship. If a similar situation arises in the future, what can you do differently?

9. Read Deuteronomy 32:35 (NIV1984): "It is mine to avenge; I will repay." What does God say about vengeance?

10. Should all people get what they deserve? Why or why not?

_____

_____

_____

_____

_____

Wrap-Up

Today we have learned how self-love is the key to loving God and loving others. One way to love others is to be kind, to make ourselves useful to someone else. Loving others well also includes controlling our anger and not seeking vengeance on those who have done us wrong.

Let's close our time together in prayer. Here are some ideas from this session that can guide our conversation with God:

- Thank God for teaching us how to love through the love He has shown us.
- Confess a commitment to be kind to strangers and those close to you.
- Ask the Holy Spirit to expose any areas of uncontrolled anger and forgive you for allowing that emotion to overcome you.
- Surrender any vengeful thoughts or behaviors you have toward someone. Thank God for being in control of the situation.

Prepare for the Next Session

Before the group meets again, read chapters 8, 9, 10 and 11 in *Love Like You've Never Been Hurt*.

BETWEEN SESSIONS

Personal Reflection

1. Choose to love yourself. Choose to see yourself the way God does. Meditate on the following verses. What can you learn from these truths?

   • I am a child of God, and I belong to Him.

   > But as many as received Him, to them He gave the right to become children of God, to those who believe in His name.
   >
   > John 1:12

   • God chose me.

   > He chose us in Him before the foundation of the world, that we should be holy and without blame before Him in love.
   >
   > Ephesians 1:4

   • Nothing can separate me from God's love.

   > For I am persuaded that neither death nor life, nor angels nor principalities nor powers, nor things present nor things to come, nor height nor depth, nor any other created thing, shall be able to separate us from the love of God which is in Christ Jesus our Lord.
   >
   > Romans 8:38–39

   • I am a new creation.

   > If anyone is in Christ, he is a new creation; old things have passed away; behold, all things have become new.
   >
   > 2 Corinthians 5:17

   • I am forgiven.

   > If we confess our sins, He is faithful and just to forgive us our sins and to cleanse us from all unrighteousness.
   >
   > 1 John 1:9

- God created me to do good works.

> For we are His workmanship, created in Christ Jesus for good works, which God prepared beforehand that we should walk in them.
>
> Ephesians 2:10

Memorize as many verses as you can, so that when you feel tempted to believe the lies of the enemy, you can combat them with truth.

_____

_____

_____

_____

_____

_____

2. You will find evidence (or not) of the Holy Spirit's work in your inner life when someone says something you do not like or agree with, is emotionally distant or has a negative attitude. Do you respond in kind, or do you respond with kindness? If your spouse has had a hard day at work and comes home with a not-so-nice attitude, do you give him or her space to wind down, or do you make passive aggressive comments? How about the atheist at work who constantly makes rude comments about your lack of intelligence for believing something that can't be proven? Do you give him an attitude or criticize his beliefs?

Check yourself. This is important: Ask the Holy Spirit to keep you in check. Anger can cloud our judgment and provoke us to make irrational and hurtful decisions that we regret. When stresses pile up, it is especially important to make time for God. Ask the Holy Spirit to reveal your weak spots. Pray for God to heal any open wounds. Pray for God to help you keep your mouth shut. Pray for God to help you walk away. Pray for God to help you wherever possible to keep the peace.

Determine today to be a peace manufacturer in your home, in the office, on your campus, in your church, in your community. Make peace where there is none. You may have conflict around you, but don't let it get in you. Remember, peacemakers put out fires, they don't start them.

Write down two current opportunities in your life to begin bringing peace instead of conflict.

_____

_____

_____

_____

_____

_____

_____

_____

_____

_____

Personal Action

1. Commit to doing one act of kindness each day for the next 21 days. It does not have to be a grand gesture. It does not have to cost anything. And you do not have to share it with the world. Give the waitress at the restaurant a generous tip. Pray a blessing over the parent who cuts in front of you in the school drop-off line. Invite the newcomer at church out to lunch. Pray for God to open your eyes and show you opportunities to show kindness to others.

2. If you have been through something particularly hurtful and are struggling with wanting to get even with someone, think about this: When Jesus was dying on the cross, staring into a crowd of people who had screamed for His death and at the soldiers who had tortured Him, He said, "Father, forgive them, for they do not know what they do" (Luke 23:34). This is one of the most powerful prayers we can pray. When you are tempted to want someone to, as they say, get as good as they gave, pray this prayer.

Give God your anger. You are not asking Him to do what He does not want to do. He has already established that He will be strong on your behalf. God will take care of the situation in His way and in His timing. He just wants you to trust Him.

BUILD UP AND FIGHT FOR YOUR MARRIAGE AND FAMILY

Big Idea for This Session

Perfect people do not make it out of the valley of marital or family trouble. The ones that do have been through hell, but through the grace of God they have declared, "I will fight for my marriage. I will fight for my family. I will fight for what's left."

Session Start-Up

Being married and raising a family is not an easy journey. There are times it feels like riding a roller coaster. Some days are filled with bliss, joy and fun. Then there are moments when you want to scream and pull your hair out. And let's not forget the seasons that bring unexpected turns or obstacles, leaving you broken and in tears.

It seems we must fight harder than ever to keep our sanity and peace in the home. Statistics tell us that half of marriages end in divorce. Families are faced with difficult challenges—addictions, pornography, even suicide. Just keeping a marriage or family from falling apart can be a struggle. Why does this happen?

The enemy desires to cause division in the family. He knows that "if a house is divided against itself, that house cannot stand" (Mark 3:25). A united family is like a strong army that can combat anything that comes against it. Division and strife, on the other hand, will weaken and destroy the foundation of a home.

So how do we prevent or overcome division among our loved ones?

You may be surprised by my answer: fight. Fight for your family. Fight to keep the peace. Fight to bring unity. Fight against thoughts of divorce, depression and rebellion. Fight for a miracle. Fight for what's left. Fight for the ones you love, because they are worth it. The Bible tells us, "Yet in all these things we are more than conquerors through Him who loved us" (Romans 8:37). The *New Living Translation* puts it this way: "Despite all these things, overwhelming victory is ours through Christ, who loved us."

If you want a marriage and family that endures the tough times, build your spiritual home. When you make Jesus your priority, you will be equipped for battle.

I realize all of you reading this participant's guide are in different seasons in your lives. You might be recently married or recently divorced. Maybe you are single and have no children, or you are a single parent. Perhaps you have never been married and have no kids. Although this session brings couples and families to the forefront, anyone reading this can answer or contemplate most of the questions. If you are single, use this opportunity to learn from those in your group who are or have been married, and look for ways to use these principles in your other relationships. These questions can also help you reflect on how to build a strong foundation for your future marriage and family, should that be your path. If you do not have kids, use these prompts to help you guide a child you mentor or a niece or nephew who is part of your life.

Talk about It

What is one key that makes marriages and families successful?

Video Session 4

Watch video session 4. While viewing the video, use the space below to record key ideas or any thoughts you want to remember.

Video Teaching Notes

There is a door of hope in the valley of marital trouble.

Marriage does not make you who you are; it reveals who you are.

A committed and lasting marriage demands a made-up mind.

It is better to be reconciled than to be right.

God is calling us to be Monuments Men and Women because our families are our treasure, our spouses are our treasure, our children are our treasure.

The miracle is not in what you lost but in what you have left.

_____

_____

_____

_____

_____

_____

_____

_____

Video Discussion

1. Do you see your family—your parents, siblings, spouse, children—as treasures? What are some ways you can protect them?

2. Nehemiah 4:2 (NLT) talks about the Israelites rebuilding the walls of Jerusalem from dust and burned stones. "Do they actually think they can make something of stones from a rubbish heap—and charred ones at that?" Do not throw away the stones that have been burned. God uses burned stones. Has God ever restored a broken relationship in your circle? Talk about it.

3. In Revelation 2:4, God rebukes the church in Ephesus for leaving their first love. He then tells them to repent and "do the first works" (verse 5). What "first works" can you do to restart the heart of your marriage when it has lost steam?

Small-Group Discussion

1. What would you say is the goal of a Christian marriage?

2. From pornography addiction to digital technology to packed schedules, what do you think is the biggest threat to maintaining healthy marriages and families? How can we overcome it?

3. What would you consider a particularly challenging experience in your marriage or as a parent, and how did you navigate through it? What did you learn about yourself in the process? What did you learn about God?

4. Earlier you read that half of marriages end in divorce. While this statistic is often said to be as true of Christian marriages as it is for non-Christian ones, author and researcher Shaunti Feldhahn discovered something astonishing. She learned that couples who attend church have a 25 to 50 percent lower divorce rate than those who do not.* Wow! That's encouraging! What are you doing to grow your faith together as a couple? If you are not married and wish to be, what are some practices you can establish with your future spouse to ensure your marriage endures?

5. In *Love Like You've Never Been Hurt*, I share how, in the Old Testament, after a high priest passed away, his garments would be handed down to his descendants so they could be ordained and anointed in them. According to 1 Peter 2:9, we—meaning every believer in Christ—are a "royal priesthood." What kind of spiritual garment (truths, principles or practices) are you passing down to the next generation?

6. Why will putting God at the forefront of your life better your relationship with your spouse or your children? Can you give an example of this truth in action?

*Shaunti Feldhahn, "Restoring Our Faith in Marriage," *Christianity Today*, August 20, 2014, http://www.christianitytoday.com/women/2014/august/restoring-our-faith-in-marriage.html.

7. Are there issues in your family that seem too overwhelming to conquer on your own? Like Nehemiah and the Jewish people who defied their enemies and rebuilt the wall around Jerusalem, what can you do to fight for your family, starting today?

_____

_____

_____

_____

_____

_____

_____

_____

_____

_____

_____

_____

Bonus Questions

8. Have you been fast with your words and slow with your actions? Have you said much and listened little? It is hard to take back the sting of name calling and insults. But it is equally hard to take back prolonged periods of silence. How can you change the way you talk to your spouse or your children?

9. Give three positive characteristics of your parents and family when you were growing up. How do you model (or hope to) any of these traits in your own family today?

10. Whether you are married or divorced, what is the biggest lesson you have learned from your relationship with your spouse or ex-spouse? If you have children, what truths have you come to realize through caring for them?

_____

_____

_____

_____

_____

_____

Wrap-Up

Today we have learned that while creating and maintaining healthy marriages and families can be quite the challenge, when we keep God at the center of our lives, He will work all things together for good. It is important to develop a relationship with Him so He can mold us to be the spouses or the parents He has created us to be. Let's close our time together in prayer. Here are some ideas from this session that can guide our conversation with God:

- Thank God that for each trial we go through, we have the opportunity to grow and be more like Jesus.
- Ask God to help you set the spiritual atmosphere in your home, to be an example your loved ones can learn from and imitate.
- Pray for God to release you of any hurts you may be holding on to from your spouse, your children or even your ex-husband or ex-wife.
- Thank God for fighting for you and your loved ones, particularly if you are going through a tough season. Thank Him in advance for sending peace during that storm.

Prepare for the Next Session

Before the group meets again, read chapter 12 in *Love Like You've Never Been Hurt*.

BETWEEN SESSIONS

Personal Reflection

1. You've heard that "opposites attract." Well, it's also true that after being married some time, opposites irritate. They are sure to cause some heated arguments and strong differences of opinion. Part of what true love means is realizing just how different you are from your spouse and growing beyond tolerating each other to appreciating those differences. Through this, you come to realize you really are better together!

   If you are married, list three differences between you and your spouse. Then write down the positive impact those differences make on you as an individual and on your marriage. If you are not married, think about how being different from another can bring two people closer or balance them out for the better.

2. Life is busy—for all of us. Being a pastor is not my only role. Being the father of five and grandfather of two plus the responsibilities that come with our ministry keep my schedule pretty full. And, like you, I can get consumed by the cares of this world. I am often asked how I prioritize my family amidst everything I am blessed to be able to do.

   I have learned to keep the main thing the main thing. Of course, my number one priority is serving and loving God. Family is next. I invest in my wife and my kids and grandchildren. I always take their calls. I spend time with them. I try not to allow life to dictate the priority of my family.

   Make a list of your top three priorities in life. Be honest with your answers. Take some time and think about what you wrote down. Ask God if you need to make any changes in your life to keep the main thing the main thing.

Personal Action

We have talked about fighting for your loved ones a lot in this session. But what does this really mean in a practical sense? Below are seven steps you can take, starting today, to begin to battle for the ones you love.

1. *Pray.* Prayer is a strong weapon. Speak life into your situation. Pray that it will turn around for your good.
2. *Read and meditate on the Bible.* "For the word of God is living and powerful, and sharper than any two-edged sword, piercing

even to the division of soul and spirit, and of joints and marrow, and is a discerner of the thoughts and intents of the heart" (Hebrews 4:12). Believe in the promises that God has written in His Word. Post them on your mirror or in your phone or other digital device to remind yourself regularly of them.

3. *Fast.* God tells us in His Word, "'Turn to Me with all your heart, with fasting, with weeping, and with mourning.' So rend your heart, and not your garments" (Joel 2:12–13). Fasting is nothing more than abstaining from food to draw closer to God. It is about submitting our minds, bodies and spirits to almighty God. You can fast all day or part of the day; you can even embark on Daniel's fast. Check out www.JentezenFranklin.org for fasting resources.

4. *Stop arguing and start listening.* Instead of picking fights or having knock-down, drag-out arguments to make a point, listen instead. It will help you understand your spouse and his or her behavior and actions. This can help resolve conflict. Proverbs 18:13 (NIV) warns, "To answer before listening—that is folly and shame."

5. *Communicate.* Lack of communication causes friction and can increase arguments. Talking helps us to understand one another better. Don't shut down. Share with your loved ones. Ask them about their day. Be positive and affirming in your speech.

6. *Say, "I love you."* This is exceptionally important. Remind your family how much you care about them. Spend time with them. Eat with them. Call them if they live far away.

7. *Forgive.* We all sin. We all mess up. We all make cruel comments. We all do stupid things. We all make mistakes. So, forgive—all the time. It's time to join the 70 × 7 club.

Where are your footprints leading your children? Your marriage? Friend, there is no better time than right now to build up your family. Do not give up the fight. We may not have answers. We may not know what the future holds. But God does. And He will fight for us. What a great promise to live under!

LOVE GOD EVEN WHEN IT HURTS

Big Idea for This Session

Whatever you are going through, whatever loss you have experienced or pain you feel in your heart, this is no time to quit the faith. Don't give up on God, because He will never give up on you.

Session Start-Up

By now you have discovered that life is full of highs and lows. It is easy to love and serve God when life is running smoothly. When you're stuck in a valley, however, it gets a bit harder to do.

Have you ever thought to yourself, *My life story isn't supposed to read like this!*? Chapters added without your consent. A dream you worked hard to accomplish crushed. A bliss-filled marriage crumbling out of nowhere. Maybe even the loss of a child.

Being at the bottom can be overwhelming, heartbreaking and terrifying. It is the petri dish Satan uses to sidetrack us from our destinies. And often it works. When your spirit is crushed, it can be paralyzing . . . but only if you let it. Like a seed, it is in our brokenness that true life blossoms. I love how *The Message* puts Psalms 51:17: "I learned God-worship when my pride was shattered. Heart-shattered lives ready for love don't for a moment escape God's notice."

You may find yourself this very day in the midst of a valley. Your life story may have taken an unforeseen, turbulent turn and you are left in its wake, winded, wounded and heartbroken. Let me encourage you that even when all seems hopeless, "all things work together for good to those who love God, to those who are the called according to His purpose" (Romans 8:28).

Sometimes it is hard to love God in our tough seasons because it seems that heaven is silent. You might assume that if you cannot feel His presence or if He is not speaking to your heart, God is mad at you. Maybe you think He has even abandoned you. This could not be further from the truth. That is not how God operates! As a fellow sojourner in the valley, I can tell you that I know He who has promised is faithful. Always faithful.

God is still God even in the unbearable seasons of life.

You may have lost a loved one in a tragic accident or by suicide. You may have gotten a bad report from a doctor. These are the seasons when God will move, work and act on your behalf. This unbearable place can bear amazing fruit later if you will just trust Him and stay faithful. Keep praising. Keep worshiping. Keep believing. Keep loving. Some of the God's best work and biggest turnarounds happen right up against the gates of hell.

Talk about It

Why is it so hard to trust God when unbearable times fall upon us?

Session 5 Video

Watch video session 5. While viewing the video, use the space below to record key ideas or any thoughts you want to remember.

Video Teaching Notes

God may not give you an explanation, but He will always give you a promise.

God knows how to make sense out of the tragedies and traumas of life.

God puts to use what He puts you through.

The pain you feel is the pain you can heal.

When bad becomes unbearable, good things are going to happen.

The greatest act of faith is not in getting the miracle. The greatest act of faith is when you can say, "God, I trust you when I don't understand a thing You're doing in my life. I still believe in you."

Video Discussion

1. Why do good people suffer bad things?

2. Is there a difference between loving God like we've never been hurt and trusting Him when we are going through hurt?

3. When tragedy or crisis strikes, many of us begin to lean toward temptation, toward anger, toward giving up. Where, or on whom, do you lean?

Small-Group Discussion

1. On pages 183–188 in *Love Like You've Never Been Hurt*, I tell the story of Wayne Caston and his family. On their way to church on Easter morning in 2007, this precious family of five was involved in a car accident that injured each family member and killed Wayne's oldest son, Charles.

   Wayne told me, "Through this tragedy, my wife and I have grown closer to God. We've had to stay connected to Him. I don't think we had a choice. I can truly say that I trust God now more than I ever have. . . . I know I will see Charles again. And I will be with him in heaven longer than I was with him down here on earth."

   Wayne's wife, Debbie, said this: "God never promised bad things wouldn't happen. But He did promise to walk with us through the tough times. Even though our lives have changed forever, God's love is forever. I draw strength from Him each day."

How does this couple's faith through their unimaginable loss encourage you in light of what you are going through?

2. Share a time when you prayed for God to perform a miracle or fix a situation and He either stepped in later or did not. How did it grow or strengthen your faith?

3. After Job lost his wealth and his health, and after his friends and his wife turned on him, he said something powerful: "Though He slay me, yet will I trust Him" (Job 13:15). After losing everything, the only thing Job had left was his faith. In saying these words, Job was holding on to the truth that, despite the heartache of life, God is still loving, still faithful and still good. If you have been through an experience in which you lost much, how did you cling to your faith?

4. When times get tough and we are struggling to make it on our own, God often brings people into our lives who can prop us up. Who has been such a person for you? Whom have you propped up lately?

5. The Bible tells us that God inhabits the praises of His people (see Psalm 22:3). There is just something about the power of praise. When we are in the valley, we must keep praising the Lord. How can you make worship intentional outside of church?

6. How does being a follower of Jesus help and equip us when tough times come?

7. God does not take away all our troubles—at least not as quickly as we would like Him to—but He does promise us peace during them. Share a time when you experienced the inexplicable peace of God.

Bonus Questions

8. When you feel God is absent in your suffering, what Scripture promise(s) can you meditate on to remind yourself that you can still trust Him?

9. What is one way you can illustrate your love for God during a tough season?

10. Based on what you learned in this session, how can you encourage someone who is struggling through an unbearable time?

Wrap-Up

Today we have learned that we can still love and trust God when the world feels like it is shattering before our eyes. Let's close in prayer. Here are some ideas from this session that can guide our conversation with God:

- Thank God for being Lord over all—over what you've lost and over what you've got left.
- Pray for Him to release a special anointing over your life that will work a miracle in and around you.
- Ask God to use your suffering for a greater purpose and to draw you nearer to Him than ever before.
- Thank Him for sending the Holy Spirit and even other people into your life to encourage you even when you feel God is silent. And thank Him for helping you stand strong during your toughest season.

Prepare for the Next Session

Before the group meets again, read chapters 13 and 14 in *Love Like You've Never Been Hurt*.

BETWEEN SESSIONS

Personal Reflection

As I was writing this guide, I was reminded of something that happened many years ago. Take your time reading this story. Pray that God speaks to your heart through these words.

More than 22 years ago, I had a dream on a Saturday night that I was attending the funeral of a child. When I walked up to the tiny casket and looked in, I was devastated to see my three-year-old daughter lying lifeless inside. I woke from the dream and immediately awakened Cherise. We began to pray for our family. We wept as the strong presence of the Lord entered our bedroom.

The next morning, still shaken by this experience, I went to church to preach a sermon titled "Cancel the Devil's Assignment." At the end of the message, I tearfully told the congregation about my dream. I explained that I believed God was warning me that Satan had targeted our children at a young age, but through the blood of Jesus Christ, we could cancel the devil's assignment in their lives. It was one of the most moving services I have ever taken part in, as fathers and mothers began to cry out to God on behalf of their families. Yet God had an even more specific plan in store.

The next day our family was scheduled to leave for a vacation at Disney World. Rather strangely, to me, Cherise begged to leave that Sunday, right after the morning services, so we could visit SeaWorld first. We decided to go even though it had not been on our itinerary.

While we were at SeaWorld, a severe thunderstorm broke out. A streak of lightning hit the top of a nearby hotel, setting it on fire. Stricken with panic, five thousand people rushed up the steps of the stadium we were in, seeking shelter from the storm. Total chaos ensued. In the midst of everything, our youngest daughter ran right past my wife to a total stranger standing nearby. The stranger, a 26-year-old woman, reached down and picked her up without hesitation, sobbing uncontrollably as she held our three-year-old daughter tight.

We were worried, and we asked the young woman's parents, who were standing nearby and were overcome with emotion, what was going on. "Two months ago," the woman's mother said, "my daughter's three-year-old child died of congestive heart failure in the middle of the night. This is the first time we have been able to get our daughter out of her bedroom because she has been so devastated with grief. She's been blaming God for taking her little girl."

I told the young mother who was holding my daughter about the prophetic dream I had preached about the previous day, and that God had brought us to SeaWorld that day to let her know that her precious daughter is with Him in heaven. I went on to tell her that our three-year-old had never run into the arms of a complete stranger. "This is a sign from God to show you how much He loves you," I said. The young woman was overwhelmed with tears. The experience restored her faith in God and brought a measure of healing of her grief.

Think of it: Out of thousands of people at SeaWorld that day, God put us in the right place, at the right time. He used us to send a message to a grieving mother to encourage her not to give up.

Be still for a few minutes. Give God space to speak to your heart.

Personal Action

You might be mad at God because you hurt so badly. You might feel weak in your faith. Maybe you have hesitated to spend time with Him because of this. Spend the next ten minutes writing out a prayer to God. Share your heart. Be open and honest. Ask Him to remind you of His unfailing love. Ask Him to remind you that you can trust Him. End your prayer by listing three things you can praise Him for, no matter how badly you hurt.

RESTART YOUR HEART

Big Idea for This Session

The enemy may be striving to destroy your life or your family, but heaven is fighting for you today. Trust God and stay in the fight. Healing and wholeness will come.

Session Start-Up

Strongholds are real. These are places in your life where the enemy has taken a seat of authority. You might be struggling with a stronghold of bitterness, unforgiveness, negativity, anger or any of the many things that prevent you from living a full life. For God to restart our hearts and heal our hearts, these strongholds must come down.

It is never easy to get to the place of victory, but through God's power, we can break the chains of whatever binds us. A word of encouragement: The greatest anointing in your life is released in the place of great struggle. When strongholds come down, God reveals His presence and victory is unleashed.

The enemy may be whispering in your heart that you will never get past your mistakes, the offenses of others, the shame or hurt you carry in your heart, the feuds that seem to gain more power in your family each passing day. Know this: Victory comes with the cross.

Through the power of the cross, you can take down strongholds. Through the power of the cross, you can defeat the enemy. Through the power of the cross, you can claim victory. Through the power of the cross, you can be healed. Through the power of the cross, you can find deliverance. Through the power of the cross, you can be set free. Ephesians 3:20 tells us that God "is able to do exceedingly abundantly above all that we ask or think, according to the power that works in us." This should encourage you not to quit.

Winston Churchill observed, "The nose of the bulldog has been slanted backwards so that he can breathe without letting go."* I love this picture of tenacity. It is a reminder to us all to continue to press in to God and hold on in the midst of a storm. It is the mindset that says, "I don't care what happens, I'm not quitting this marriage. I'm not quitting my family. I'm not quitting what I believe God will restore, redeem and rebuild!"

Be encouraged and stay in the fight. Good news—God has already won! He is speaking this promise to you today: "No weapon formed against you shall prosper, and every tongue which rises against you in judgment you shall condemn. This is the heritage of the servants of the LORD, and their righteousness is from Me" (Isaiah 54:17).

Invite God to bring healing and wholeness in your heart today. Ask Him to help you conquer every area in your life and begin to live victoriously.

Talk about It

What are some important habits and disciplines we can practice to develop perseverance and never give up when tough times come?

*The International Churchill Society, "Churchill Quotes: 'One-Liners'," accessed November 30, 2017, https://www.winstonchurchill.org/resources/quotes/churchill-one -liner-quotes/.

Video Session 6

Watch video session 6. While viewing the video, use the space below to record key ideas or any thoughts you want to remember.

Video Teaching Notes

Love never fails.

If you will not quit, you cannot lose.

Don't settle for less than the best.

God's grace is able to do exceedingly abundantly above all that we can ask or think.

Your destiny is greater than your difficulty.

The King has one more move.

Video Discussion

1. Have you ever settled for the "Uganda Plan"—something that was less than what God wanted for your life? What was the outcome?

2. What is one thing you can do today to begin to reconnect with someone whom you have written off? (For example, call or give an invitation to lunch.)

3. What does it mean for God to restart your heart?

Small-Group Discussion

1. Name a stronghold that God has revealed through the course of working through this participant's guide.

2. The apostle Paul wrote, "For though we walk in the flesh, we do not war according to the flesh. For the weapons of our warfare are not carnal but mighty in God for pulling down strongholds"

(2 Corinthians 10:3–4). What weapons, according to Scripture, must we fight the enemy with?

3. In *Love Like You've Never Been Hurt*, I explain that there is one thing that you and I can do that God cannot—we can reach the end of our resources. God has never done all that He can do. He has always got one more move.

    Share an experience in which God performed the impossible after you prayed about a desperate situation.

4. How is Jesus our ultimate example of going through unimaginable difficulty and not giving up?

5. Did you know that over half of all birds in New Zealand cannot fly? It's because they have no predators. Before humans inhabited this island, no predatory mammals existed there. The main threats were other birds, so it was safer to stay on the ground. Think about this: Without the opposition of offenses, you will never mount up with wings like an eagle (see Isaiah 40:31). How has opposition afforded you something in return (e.g., a victory, growth in character or a deeper faith in God)?

6. How can you strengthen your faith today to believe that God can heal your heart, reconcile a relationship or overcome a stronghold of unforgiveness?

7. We read in 2 Corinthians 6:1–3 (MESSAGE),

    > Please don't squander one bit of this marvelous life God has given us. God reminds us, I heard your call in the nick of time; the day you needed me, I was there to help. Well, now is the right time to listen, the day to be helped. Don't put it off.

    I like to think of us as day traders. Some use their time wisely, focusing on becoming the people God wants them to be. Others trade the fullness of their lives for something that may not matter, like pride or a grudge. Are you living life full throttle? Discuss any changes you need to make to set your heart on the right things.

_____

_____

_____

_____

_____

_____

_____

_____

_____

_____

Bonus Questions

8. I write in *Love Like You've Never Been Hurt*,

   Two words at the beginning of Job 42:16 have tremendous impact. "After this Job lived one hundred and forty years, and saw his children and grandchildren for four generations." Job had gone through crises of catastrophic proportions. He lost his family, his health, his wealth. Everything. But God gave him an "after this."

   Share an "after this" in your own life.

9. Share a change of heart you've made or that others have seen in your life since you first started reading this participant's guide. How can you continue in this pattern of renewal?

10. What is the most meaningful truth you have learned while reading this book? How will you commit to living out this truth each day going forward?

_____

_____

_____

_____

_____

Wrap-Up

My hope is that today you have been encouraged to know that no matter what has happened in the past, there can be a wonderful ending—an "after this" of change, of renewal, of healing, of purpose. God is not through with you yet. No matter how hard the enemy may have tried to gain territory in your life, you can stand strong in your faith knowing God is on your side. Let's close our time together in prayer. Here are some ideas from this session that can guide our conversation with God:

- Ask God to release His power and remove any stronghold in your heart or in your family.
- Confess that the blood of Jesus sets you free, that you are climbing higher than your situation, that you will no longer live in the place of defeat.
- Thank God for giving you the spirit of a warrior through His power, so that no matter how hurt you have been, you will not quit.
- Give Him praise for setting you free, for giving you the victory, for transforming your heart. You will never be the same again!

AFTER THE SESSION

Personal Reflection

1. As we close this book, take your time digesting and meditating on these final thoughts. I believe God has been speaking to you. And I believe that you have been listening and taking heed of His voice. As you finish reading this final session, have faith that a new you, a new life, a new heart is emerging. When you start getting discouraged or allow old habits or reminders of past hurts to creep in, remember the following truths:

   • God has a purpose for your life. "For I know the thoughts that I think toward you, says the LORD, thoughts of peace and not of evil, to give you a future and a hope" (Jeremiah 29:11).

   • God is always faithful. "Therefore know that the LORD your God, He is God, the faithful God who keeps covenant and mercy for a thousand generations with those who love Him and keep His commandments" (Deuteronomy 7:9).

   • God will do what He does best—turn your difficult seasons into an amazing testimony of deliverance and His faithfulness! "And we know that all things work together for good to those who love God, to those who are the called according to His purpose" (Romans 8:28).

   • God is a finisher. "[I am] confident of this very thing, that He who has begun a good work in you will complete it until the day of Jesus Christ" (Philippians 1:6). Whatever change is happening in your heart will continue if you persevere and allow God to work within you.

2. Read the following passage of Scripture in Isaiah 43:16–19 (MESSAGE):

This is what GOD says, the God who builds a road right through the ocean, who carves a path through pounding waves, the God who summons horses and chariots and armies—they lie down and then can't get up; they're snuffed out like so many candles: "Forget about what's happened; don't keep going over old history. Be alert, be present. I'm about to do something brand-new. It's bursting out! Don't you see it? There it is! I'm making a road through the desert, rivers in the badlands."

Allow these words to recharge you. God has something new in store for you—and it will only come when you refuse to quit.

Personal Action

If the enemy can convince you that your best days are behind you . . . he wins. For "where there is no vision, the people perish" (Proverbs 29:18 KJV)—and dead people can do nothing for God.

But you're not dead. You're alive. Encouraged. Strengthened. Uplifted. You know God loves you and will not fail you. You know He has a plan for your life. And you know He will bring healing, hope and wholeness.

Write down a declaration of faith. List areas of negativity, bitterness and unforgiveness that He has helped you discern through reading this book. Decide within your heart to keep those spaces clean and clear. Finally, declare over your life that as long as you have any say in it, these strongholds are no longer welcome in your life or in your house!

Use the following affirmations to jumpstart this process, but personalize them. Make these declarations your own. Add names of people if you choose (e.g., "I am never going to quit loving [insert name]."). You can even choose some of the Bible verses we have talked about in this guide and declare them over your life. Say out loud these confessions daily, or as much as you need to.

I am never going to quit loving.

I am never going to quit serving.

I am never going to quit forgiving.

I am never going to quit praying.

I am never going to quit believing.

I am never going to quit being kind.

I am never going to quit serving God.

I am never going to quit loving like I've never been hurt.

Friend, I believe God is, indeed, doing something brand-new in your life!

Notes

Notes

Jentezen Franklin is the senior pastor of Free Chapel, a multicampus church. Each week his television program, *Kingdom Connection*, is broadcast on major networks all over the world. A *New York Times* bestselling author, Jentezen has written eight books, including the groundbreaking *Fasting*; *Right People, Right Place, Right Plan*; and *Fear Fighters*.

Jentezen and his wife, Cherise, have been married thirty years. They have five children and two grandchildren and make their home in Gainesville, Georgia.